# CURLING

## ... FUN FOR EVERYONE

### Dar Curtis

**Coachwhip Publications**

Greenville, Ohio

*Curling ... Fun for Everyone,* by Dar Curtis
Copyright © 2013 Coachwhip Publications
No claims made on public domain material.
Published 1959.

ISBN 1-61646-188-8
ISBN-13 978-1-61646-188-1

CoachwhipBooks.com

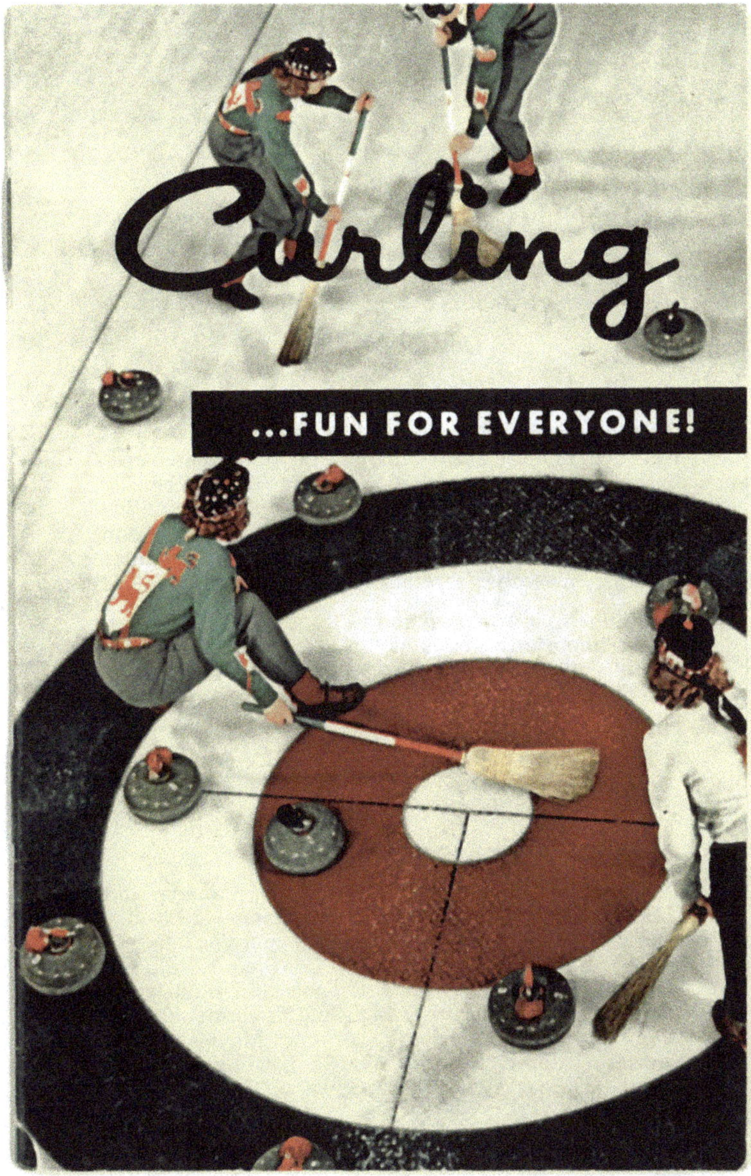
Curling
...FUN FOR EVERYONE!

# CURLING

## . . . FUN FOR EVERYONE

By

### DAR CURTIS

#### FOREWORD

Unique is this age old sport of curling in that it is free of commercialism and has no professionals. It has enough interest so that one never thinks of betting on the outcome of a game. It is the only competitive sport in which all members of the family, young and old, can participate during the five long winter months, November through March.

This book is intended to briefly give the novice all of the important phases of the game, and it is hoped that it will help, if only in a small way, to make curling one of the major winter sports on the North American Continent.

The splendid help of The Macdonald Tobacco Company and Ken Watson of Canada, in the preparation of this booklet, is greatly appreciated.

#### CONTENTS

Fourth Printing

# A BRIEF HISTORY OF CURLING

THE ORIGIN of this little known but grand old game is a bit vague. Some believe it had it's beginning as "child's play" on the frozen ponds and streams of the Continent. Others insist that the "roaring game" is Scottish through and through. With words such as "bonspiel," meaning good play, "channelstane," "hack," "hog" etc., one would say that the continentals had an argument. On the other hand, it is a known fact that the fascinating game of curling appeared in Scotland in the early sixteenth century as evidenced by a curling stone, bearing the date of 1511, which was unearthed near Stirling. There is also evidence that, at about that time, the inhabitants of Kilsyth formed one of the first curling organizations, followed soon after by other clubs. It was not until 1760, however, that the famous Edinburgh Cannonmills Club was established. Both Robert Burns and Sir Walter Scott refer to the game as the "manly Scottish exercise."

In 1838 the Grand Caledonian Curling Club was formed for the sole purpose of fixing standardized rules of the game for use wherever curling was played. This organization is still in existence, but is now known as the Royal Caledonian Curling Club, having been granted this title by Her Majesty the Queen in the year 1843. All of the important curling clubs of the world, through their local associations, are affiliated with this "Mother Club."

Several other countries enjoy the sport such as Switzerland, where there are upwards of 60 clubs. Here in the highest altitudes, keen, natural, out-of-door ice is found, especially during the months of December and January. England, Sweden, Norway, France, Italy, Austria, New Zealand and even China also have curling clubs.

1

IN CANADA the game has flourished since the beginning of the 19th Century when the Scottish regiments found themselves in Quebec where the climate in the wintertime was such that it could be played on the frozen lakes and rivers. Because of the difficulty of obtaining granite stones from Scotland, cast iron "stones" made from melted down cannon balls were used. Up until 1955 "irons" were still popular. In fact many of the natives preferred them over granites.

The Royal Montreal Curling Club, organized in 1807, confines it's activities to curling only and has the distinction of being the oldest club for any kind of sport on the North American Continent. Curling now thrives in all Provinces of the Dominion, there being over 2500 curling clubs where some 500,000 men, women and children enjoy the sport. There are more curlers than golfers and about 80,000 school children throughout the country play the game at schools and on municipal ice rinks.

Many of Canada's principal cities have "pay-as-you-play" establishments similar to our bowling alleys.

The most significant of all annual events in the world of Curling is, undoubtedly, the Canadian Championships which were inaugurated in 1927 under the sponsorship of the Macdonald Tobacco Company. Throughout each season, playdowns are held to determine the eligible teams from each province to vie for the National Honors. Each season a different city is selected for the site of this exciting and colorful event, which increases in popularity each year. During the four days' play at the Regina Stadium a few years ago, over 54,000 spectators enjoyed watching the experts play. Many of the movies, generously supplied by the Macdonald organization and offered for loan as listed on the last page of this booklet, were made at these events.

IN THE UNITED STATES curling has been played since about 1830 when it crept down across the Canadian Border into The New England States and into the northern part of Michigan. The first association, known as the Grand National Curling Club of America was founded in 1867 and is still in operation. The Mid-West Curling Association was set up in 1945, shortly after the game was revived in that area, having been dormant in the Central States since about 1910. The game has spread to the Northwest and Alaska. In 1958 the U. S. Curling Association was formed. North Dakota, Washington and California also have associations.

Since the recent modernization of the game, there has been a great re-awakening of Curling in America. With the advent of the new "slide delivery," developed by **Ken Watson** * of Winnipeg, Canada and the many new artificial ice arenas throughout the country, the game is fast finding its place in the field of winter sports.

During the past several years, Chicago suburbs have shown the greatest curling growth in the country. In 1936 there were but 40 curlers in the district. Now there are over 4000 who play at nine suburban clubs, all of which have artificial ice for curling purposes only. At least 1000 of these players are women.

All who are interested in furthering the sport will benefit by subscribing to the North American Curling News which was established in 1946. Its publisher and Editor is, L. T. Kreutzig, South Milwaukee, Wisconsin.

In March 1957, using the Canadian Brier as a pattern, the first U. S. Men's Curling Championship, sponsored by Marshall Field & Company, was held at the Chicago Stadium. The champions of New Hampshire, New York, Massachusetts, Michigan, North Dakota, Minnesota, Wisconsin, Illinois, Washington, and Alaska competed. During the four days of round-robin play by the championship teams there were over 20,000 spectators. The event was generously publicized by the press and several hours were devoted to the sport by television and radio. The Minnesota team from Hibbing was the winner with Illinois represented by a rink from Chicago Curling Club, second.

In April 1958 this event was played at the beautiful Arena in Milwaukee, Wisconsin. The Michigan team from Detroit was the victor. In 1959 it was held at Green Bay, Wisconsin and again Minnesota won first place.

At Chicago in 1960, North Dakota took the honors; in 1961 Washington State at Grand Forks, N.D.; Minnesota won again at Detroit in 1962 and Michigan was the victor at Duluth in 1963.

In 1959 the Scotch Whiskey Association, footing all expenses, established the international championships known as the "Scotch Cup" matches with play each year in Scotland. The winners of the Nationals in the various countries are eligible to compete but the only nations thus far invited have been Canada, U.S.A., Sweden and, of course, Scotland.

*See his excellent book on curling pub. by Copp Clark Co., Ltd., Can.

# CURLING STONES

In the beginning, stones used for curling were a variety of sizes and shapes. Even a pair used by a single player were not matched in weight and many of them had no handles — just finger holes, as found in our modern bowling balls, served for the grip of thumb and forefinger. Most of the stones came from the bottom of streams and along the shore line of lakes the edges of which were worn smooth by the action of the water. These primitive stones were so much lighter, weighing from about 5 to 25 pounds, that the game then resembled our modern game of quoits, and sometimes would soar off the ice surface for part of the way. A stake was used to mark the target instead of circles drawn on the ice.

Later on as the game was perfected, heavier boulders were used but still the pairs were not matched in weight —some over 100 pounds, and so unwieldy that they were never lifted off of the ice during delivery.

Insertion of handles became the next step in the evolution of today's curling stone; then in about 1775 circular stones became common. Standardization had at last begun.

At present, in Canada and the U. S., all curling stones are of standard size and weight, 42½ pounds—and therefore are interchangeable. The clubs, rather than the individual curlers, own the stones, obviating the necessity of lugging one's own pair around to events at and away from home. At present stones cost about $90.00 per pair and now have running edges on both sides.

Because of the delay in getting the Scottish granites, the Canadians have developed a "stone" of plastic material (weighted to 40 lbs.). Once proven acceptable, they may become standard.

4

# HOW THE GAME IS PLAYED

*Contestants wear rubbers, or rubber soled shoes, which help them to keep their footing. Those who enter into the game actively, in an indoor rink, will find that light woolen clothing is sufficient as the inside temperature is seldom under 25°. For outdoor play, heavier garments should be worn. For freedom of action, in any case, both men and women should don loose fitting garments such as would be worn for winter-time golf. Slacks, not ski trousers, unless made of "stretch" material that are loose fitting at the knees, are a must for both men and women. (For ease of action, some women in Scotland and Canada wear skirts, but American women have fashioned slacks). Gloves or mittens are generally worn, but it is preferable for the "feel" to remove a glove before handling the stone.*

A rink (team) consists of four players each handling two stones, making a total of eight stones played by each side, or sixteen stones by both teams during an inning or 'end.' Stones are played alternately with those of the opposition.

A goal in the form of a 12 foot circle, at each end of a long narrow sheet of ice is called the "House." As in shuffle-board, an 'end' has been completed when all sixteen stones have come to rest at the end of the 'sheet'. Then for convenience, the next end is played in the opposite direction to the other goal. Any number of ends, agreed upon in advance, comprise a game. Normally 10 ends, taking about 2½ hours (15 minutes per end), are played.

At the end of the sheet from which the stones are delivered, the player uses a 'hack', or brace for his foot, fastened to the ice to keep from slipping as he swings the stone forward on it's journey down the ice.

The least experienced player, called the 'lead', generally handles the first two stones for his team, each alternately with the opposing lead. It is relatively simple for these first players to do their part when there are no other stones on the ice.

A unique feature of the game, compared to other sports like shuffle-board or ten-pen bowling wherein each player is "on his own," is that all four team-mates assist in determining the action of each stone played. For example, except while delivering his two stones, the 'skip' (captain) remains in the house at the opposite end where he can plan the strategy and direct all of the play of his team. He can better judge what is required of his

5

team-mates from that position. The two other players, with brooms ready, hurry along preceding each moving stone as it travels down the ice toward the goal.

A considerable amount of foot-work is required to keep ahead of the rather fast moving stone and they must be right there ready at all times to sweep at the command of their skip. As will be explained later, sweeping which is difficult to do well, is an essential part of the game.

After the lead has handled his two stones, alternately with the opposing lead, it is then the 'second' player's turn to perform likewise. Having finished delivering his stones, the lead moves up to take over the sweeping job with the number three player (called the 'vice-skip'). who has already helped in the sweeping of the first two lead stones for his side. In turn, the vice-skip plays his two stones alternately with the opposing team's vice-skip. His two stones are swept by the lead and the second players.

As each team takes it's turn alternately, the opposing four players "give up the ice" to the side whose stone is being played as they are not allowed to interfere in any way with the opponents' stones. The opposing skip, however, may remain in the goal, generally to the rear of the skip whose side is about to play, so that he may study the ice and the action of the stones.

**SWEEPING**—One must now understand the purpose of that all important feature of the game. A stone, which otherwise would fall short, can be "brought along" to its proper destination by accurate sweeping. A skip should be able to judge the 'weight' (speed) of a stone soon after it leaves the hand of the player. If, in his judgment, it is 'light' (not having enough momentum to do the intended job), he commands "sweep," which immediately brings the two brooms into action. The command "brooms up" is used when he thinks they have swept enough. A stone can be made to travel as much as 6 to 10 feet farther by vigorous sweeping than if it had been left alone. On the other hand, a stone which has been over-played (having too much speed) cannot be slowed up in any way. So they say, "Play 'em light and blame it on the sweepers."

A well swept stone will not arc, or curl, as much and therefore it can be made to pass a guard stone which would otherwise be nicked. Those who want a real work-out can certainly acquire it in this part of the game.

On the other hand, the "Scottish Brush" or miniature push broom (See photo—page 28) is becoming more popular every season especially among players of advanced age, or those physically unable to wield the heavier American broom. When properly used, it has been proven to be very effective.

Judging the ice is another important responsibility of the skip. No practice stones may be played before the game starts. Curling stones do not travel in a straight line. As they are delivered, they are made to revolve by a slight twist of the wrist, either to the right, called the 'in-turn'; or the left, called the 'out-turn'. The former slowly rotates the stone clock-wise, while the latter, or 'out-turn', causes a counter-clockwise movement as it moves down the ice. Because of the centrifical force of this rotary motion, the stone "pulls" in the direction in which it is turning so that the trajectory, or path of the stone, is in the form of an arc. In calling for a given play, the Skip first pats the ice with his broom indicating where he wants the stone to end up. Then, after signaling for the desired turn, by holding out his right or left arm, with his broom as a target for the player, (he holds it edge-wise), judging the amount of 'borrow' needed to have the stone reach the objective or accomplish the intended purpose. So that by the time the stone has traveled its full distance, it will have "arced" and come to rest (or struck another stone) accomplishing what the skip had in mind.

When the time comes for the skips to play the last two stones for their respective sides, there are, theoretically, 12 stones 'on the ice'. Consequently, the task is then much more difficult, calling for more skill and experienced play than before the ice has been cluttered up with stones. The vice-skip usually is called upon to hold the broom as a target, while these last stones of the skip are being played.

The most astounding, delicate shots can be performed by experienced players such as one finds in other sports like golf or billiards. It may seem strange, but curling is similar to both of these games: In curling, as in golf, there is a back swing and a follow-through, the objective being to get the right distance and direction. The stones act like billiard balls when they strike each other. Some of the typical shots found in curling are described later in this booklet.

**SCORING**—As in shuffle-board, after all 16 stones have come to rest, and the inning is finished, the score for that end is determined by the opposing vice-skips who

7

must agree or call for a referees' decision. When it is difficult to decide which stones are nearest the center, a large sized measuring device resembling a compass is used. Only one side can score in an end. As in the game of Horseshoes, only the stones that are nearest the center of the goal, count. If one side has, say, two stones nearer the center than any of the opponent's stones, the count is two, (nothing for the opponents). Sometimes, before the very last stone is played, (on the part of the side that has no stones counting) there may be three or four counters for the opponents. If the final stone of the "down-side" comes in closer than any of the former counters, the final score would be recorded as one point for the side playing this last stone.

The rule is that the winning side of an end must play the first stone of the next end, thereby giving an advantage to the side that lost the previous end. In order to determine who plays first at the beginning of a game, a coin is tossed; the winner exercises his choice, but generally plays last.

The maximum points that can be scored for a single end would, of course, be eight. Such a victory is most unusual; less frequent than a "hole in one" in golf. During the entire 28 years of my curling experience I have witnessed only two "eight ends." The late Willie Brown, who passed away in 1961, was the oldest member of the Royal Montreal Curling Club. He was an ardent curler for over sixty years. It is said that he held the world's record for this achievement, having made four "eight ends" during his career!

# CURLING CUSTOMS

A fraternal atmosphere, naturally generated through its many customs and friendly gestures, characterizes this glorious sport of curling. Hospitality and friendliness dominate the thrills of the game itself, at home and abroad, wherever it is found! Mainly, it is this special feature that brands curling as "different" from any other competitive sport.

**CURLING PIN COLLECTIONS**—The most popular hobby found among addicts of the sport is that of badge collecting. All curling clubs have their distinctive insignia on their pin, or badge. When a rink from one club has a match with another club for the first time, the players exchange pins. Many wear an array of these keep-sakes on their Glengarries or Balmorals. Such a custom helps recall good times and friendships made at home and abroad.

**"PLATE GLASS SKIPS"**—Among novices, or those who are unable to take an active part in the game, we find the "spectator fan". It is a fascinating pastime to sit behind the glass in the spectators' gallery, watch and comment on the actions of the players. It is said that "plate glass skips" never miss a shot!

**EVENTS — HERE AND THERE**—Aside from the regular games played by the women during the daytime, the men in the evening and the mixed games on the week-end, curlers like to travel. Once they have sampled the away-from-home bonspiels, they get the wanderlust habit! Such tournaments may last from one to four days, or even a week. Hospitality is thrown back and forth throughout the season.

**"FAMILY BONSPIEL"**—Of all curling events, this one, instigated by the writer at the Chicago Curling Club in 1951, is the liveliest of all. Rinks made up of father, mother and two youngsters (if you haven't got two, borrow one), enter this thrilling tournament held during the Christmas Holidays when the children are home from school. What an exciting time is had by all, players and spectators alike! In what other athletic game can people of all ages participate and thoroughly enjoy themselves?

**"BROOM STACKING"**—This is the simplest of all curling customs to master. It is best done when the tired, thirsty player leaves the ice. Instruction is unnecessary and now he can limber up that elbow which has become stiff from holding it so straight! "Broom-stacking" is the best cure for missed shots and parched throats.

9

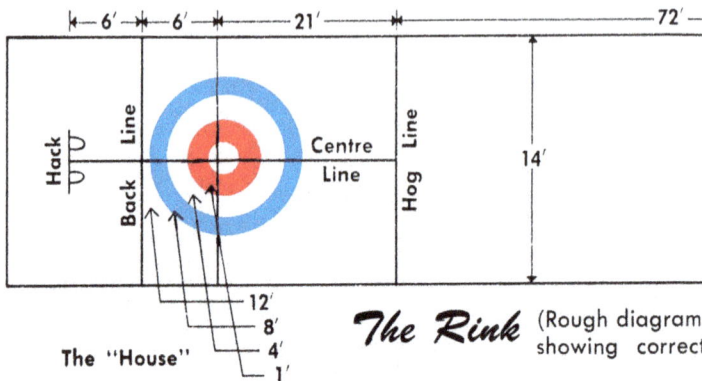

The Rink (Rough diagram showing correct

The "House"

12'
8'
4'
1'

**RULES OF THE GAME**

As Established Under the Dominion Curling Association and Adopted by the U. S. Curling Associations.
*(Summarized for brevity)*

**Rules 1-4** specify dimensions and markings of a sheet of ice.

**5** No stone shall exceed 44 lbs. in weight, including handles.

**6** Once a match starts, no stone shall be substituted for another (except under Rule 7 or 20).

**7** Should a stone break, the largest fragment shall count.

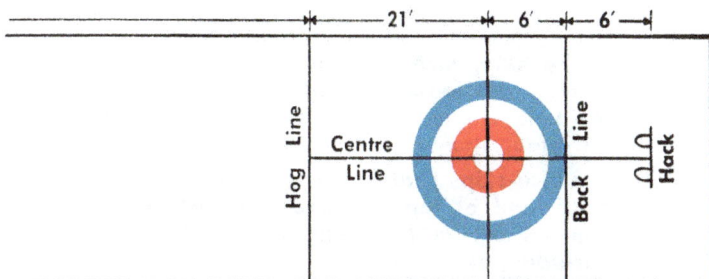

(... of rink not drawn to scale but set-up and measurements.)

"Sweeping Score" or "Tee Line"

**8** Any stone which rolls over shall be removed from play.

**9** A player must have hold of the handle to be entitled to replay the shot if the handle quits the stone in delivery. Stone may not be replayed, once delivery is started, if stone has crossed nearest sweeping line.

**10** A stone must clear the "hog line" to remain in play unless it strikes another stone first.

**11** Any stone passing clear of the "back line" is out of play.

**12** All matches shall be of a certain number of "ends" or "by time" as established at the outset. In case of a tie play shall continue until either team scores.

**13** Each rink shall consist of four players a side, each player delivering two stones alternately with his opponent. This rotation of players shall not change once the match has commenced.

**14** If the skip, vice-skip, or second player is absent, the lead shall play four stones. If the lead is absent, the second player shall play four stones.

**15** The vice-skips shall settle by lot which party shall lead at the first end after which the winners of the preceding end shall do so (including extra ends).

**16** The skip shall have control of the game for his rink, and may play any position in the game he elects, but without changing his position once the match has commenced. When his turn to play comes, he shall select one of his players to act as skip.

**17** During the course of a match players shall keep off the centre of the rink except the playing party and his sweepers.

**18** Skips and vice-skips may stand within the circle but the skip of the playing party has priority. Behind the sweeping line the privileges of both skips shall be equal.

**19** Each player must play from the hack and if, in the delivery of the stone the foot on which the player is sliding touches the nearest hog line, the stone shall be removed from the ice by the playing side.

**20** Each player must be ready to play when his turn comes. Should a player play an opponent's stone, the correct stone shall be put in its place.

If a player plays out of turn
(a) The stone may be stopped and returned to the player;

(b) If the stone completes the play and comes to rest, the missed stone shall be played by the player missing his turn as the last stone of his team for that end;

(c) If it cannot be decided who missed playing the stone, the lead shall play the last stone for his team that end.

Sweeping shall be under the direction of the skips from tee to tee but behind the tee, or sweeping line, both skips or vice-skips shall have equal rights.

(a) If a running stone be deflected by the broom of a sweeper or any of the team to whom it belongs, it shall be removed from the ice by the playing side.

(b) But if its course or position is altered by an opposing party, it shall be replaced by the skip to which it belongs.

**21** A rink shall score one point for every stone which is nearer the tee than any stone of the opposing rink. Any stone touching the outer circle is eligible. Disputed shots shall be determined by the acting skips or by the umpire or by a neutral party in that order. No measuring is allowed until the end terminates except by the umpire to decide whether or not a stone is alive.

**22** On appeal, the umpire or the committee responsible shall decide whether the ice is playable. If postponed, the match commences "de novo".

# GLOSSARY OF CURLING TERMS

**BACK BOARD**—Border at extreme end of "Sheet."

**BACK RING**—Diameter of 12 ft. circle behind the "tee."

**BACK SCORE**—Straight line, parallel to "Sweeping Score" back of circles.

**BIG END**—Score of 4 or more points in one "end."

**BITER**—Stone just touching outside circle.

**BONSPIEL** — Tournament; when a number of teams play in several events.

**CENTER LINE**—Line drawn on ice from "hack" to "hog".

**CHAP & LIE**—When played stone strikes edge of another stone and moves to another position in goal.

**CHIP**—See "wick". When played stone nicks edge of another stone.

**COUNTER**—A stone lying closer to the "tee" than any opponent's stone.

**CROSS HANDLE**—When handle of stone is held at right angles to target.

**CUP (of Stone)**—Concaved area inside the 5 inch running edge on bottom of stone.

**DRAW**—Lateral swing of stone during it's movement up the ice. (Amount of arc)

**DRAW WEIGHT**—When stone travels as far as inner rings of "house".

**END**—Inning, or division of a game, played from one end of the sheet to the other.

**FREEZE**—When stone has just enough momentum to stop when just touching another stone.

**FRONT RING**—Diameter of 12 ft. circle in front of "tee".

**GUARD**—A stone in front of another stone.

**HACK**—An immovable brace for the foot in or on ice at point of delivery. One is provided on each side of center line for right and left handed players.

**HEAD**—Goal or "house".

**HOG**—When played stone fails to clear "hog line".

**HOG LINE**—Line drawn on ice in front of goal, which stone must clear to be in play.

**HOUSE**—Goal, designated by circles. (see drawing page 10)

**IN-TURN**—Stone turning clock-wise as it travels.

**IN-WICK**—When played stone strikes inside of objective stone causing former to move toward "tee".

**LEAD**—Member of team who plays first stones for his side.

**NARROW**—Stone played "off the broom" on side between skip's broom and objective.

**OFF THE BROOM**—Stone not played toward skip's broom.

**ON THE BROOM**—Stone played directly at skip's broom.

**OUT-TURN**—Stone turning in counter-clockwise direction.

**OUT-WICK**—When played stone strikes outside of objective stone.

**OVER DRAW WEIGHT**—Stone having enough momentum to reach rings behind "tee" line.

**PAT LID**—Stone that comes to rest in center of goal.

**PEBBLE**—Roughtening of ice surface by "mist-spray" after flooding. This allows air to enter "cup" on bottom of stone.

**POCKET**—Semi-circular position of stones concentric to rings.

**POINTS GAME**—Practice game wherein typical shots are set-up, played and scored according to accuracy.

**PORT**—Opening between two stones sufficient to allow another stone to pass through.

**PROMOTION**—Hitting a stone, causing it to be advanced.

**RINK**—(Two meanings) Group of players making up team — "Sheet" of ice.

**ROCK**—Another term for "stone".

**ROLL**—Any movement of stone after striking another.

**RUB**—See "chip".

**RUNNER**—Fast moving stone—usually for a "take out".

**SECOND SHOT (Stone)**—Second stone nearest "tee".

**SHEET**—Ice area on which game is played.

**SHOT ROCK**—Stone lying closest to center of goal.

**SKIP**—Captain of team of players.

**SLIDE**—Forward movement of player delivering a stone.

**STRAIGHT HANDLE**—Stone traveling without revolving motion as in case of "in-turn" or "out-turn".

**STRIKING**—When played stone hits another stone removing it from play.

**SWEEPING SCORE**—Line drawn through center of goal at right angles to "center line".

**SWINGY ICE**—When "draw" or arc of traveling stone is greater than usual.

**TAKE OUT**—"Striking" a stone hard enough to remove it from rings. (see "Striking").

**TARGET**—Skip's broom held at goal designating direction in which stone is to be played.

**TEE**—Exact center of the goal.

**THIRD**—"Vice-Skip"—Player that delivers 3rd pair of stones for his side.

**WEIGHT**—Speed at which stone is delivered.

**WICK**—See "chip". When stone strikes edge of another stone.

**WIDE**—Stone played "off the broom", outside of skip's broom away from objective.

**WOBBLER**—Stone that rocks from side to side as it travels, because it is not resting on its running surface.

## "HACK MANNERS"

*(The following technique of stone delivery has been found to be the most successful routine for the novice. It has been prepared after twenty years of observing the behavior of over 1800 beginners on the ice for the first time.)*

A very important difference between curling and almost any other competitive sport, is that preliminary lessons and laborious practice are not required. On the very first day, without "beginner's embarrassment," one can enter into his initial game, have fun, and be a credit to his team.

This does not mean that the novice can be thrown bodily onto the ice and be expected to perform well, without any idea of how he should behave in the "hack," and what he should do with a 42 pound rock. This booklet is not intended to make an expert out of a first timer. None of our competitive sports can be learned by reading about it. So, before his first game of curling, the rank beginner should be willing to devote, say, one hour to getting the right habits fixed in mind and body. To enter a few 'ends' of play in an actual game with his teammates, immediately following this bit of required instruction, is of course, very desirable.

Handling the first two stones as "lead" for your team, is relatively simple because there are no other stones on the ice except those of the opposing lead. Complications to be met with by more experienced players, come later in the 'end'. So now let us enumerate the few essentials the beginner should strive to make habitual, right from the start.

1. **One must never go on to the ice without first wiping his feet.**

   Dirt tracked onto ice by many players impedes running of stones.

2. **While on the ice, all players carry brooms (or brushes).**

   Brooms give the players a feeling of security, like a

cane. They are used for cleaning the running edge and for sweeping stones farther. Tired Curlers use them to sit on. "Skip" uses his as target.

3. **For ease and for safety's sake, a stone is never lifted off of ice except once (during back-swing).**
   They slide along easily while riding on ice. That's why children weighing 100 pounds can handle them.

4. **Before each delivery, a stone is turned over and the running surface properly cleaned.**
   Necessary to insure smooth running of stone. A simple flip of the wrist readily turns the stone over. The broom is then used to clean the under side.

5. **While taking Skip's instructions, one stands in hack with foot in position to use back of hack for support. Only when he is sure of what is wanted does he bend knees to grasp stone's handle.**
   The standing position enables player to better see and hear skip's directions and it is less tiring to the muscles immediately before delivering stone.

6. **While standing, player should (A) Face broom and (B) Draw imaginary line to Skip's broom.**

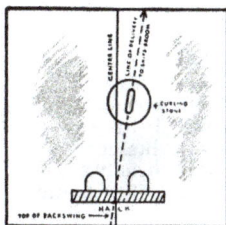

   (a) It is awkward to play stone on "imaginary line" unless player is facing skip's broom. Facing the broom is done by moving the feet. (See figure)
   (b) Before going down for stone, player can 'aim' by swinging right arm backward and forward on line with broom.

7. **In going down for stone with shoulders square on line of play, bend knees reaching for stone's handle, without taking eyes off the Skip's broom.**
   Never look down, but feel for Stone's handle. Keeping eyes fixed on 'target' through entire action, helps bring best results. Right arm should be kept straight; therefore only go down far enough to grasp handle in fingers.

**8.** **Grip handle lightly, but firmly, in fingers with thumb on top.**

Do not allow palm to touch handle throughout the entire action of delivery. Stone 'hangs' from fingers held together in center of handle, for proper balance. (See figure)

**9.** **The actual swinging of the stone is done in three rhythmical counts.**

*"One"*—With most of the weight on the right leg, slide stone forward.

*"Two"*—Swing stone to rear, slightly straightening right knee, until stone comes off ice of it's own accord. (See figure)

*"Three"*—Swing stone forward while sliding out on left foot, bending forward at the hips, straightening right leg and bending the left knee. (See figure)

Through the entire action of "Two" and "Three" above, do not take eyes off of skip's broom, nor turn handle of stone. Forget the destination of the stone. Concentrate on the skip's broom.

The above movements sound a bit complicated, but if one tries, they should come naturally; and if they are rhythmical, the proper timing will come with just a little practice. As in the case of the golf swing, "timing" is essential. Do not hurry any of the above movements. (Think of the action in slow motion pictures.)

In the beginning, it may be difficult to keep one's balance usually due to the fear of falling during the slide forward. This can be overcome through practice, and after the experience of a few falls from that short distance to the ice (if one is in proper stretched position), he discovers that it is not serious. The broom, in the left hand, lends the feeling of security; and if one places his right hand on the ice after the follow-through, the fall will be prevented. Never fall backwards (to the left), or try to stand up after the follow-through; keep the right leg stretched to the rear.

10. **Stones are always delivered with either the 'In-Turn' or the 'Out-Turn', never with a 'Straight Handle'.**

In learning, however, one should not try to put a turn on the stone until he has the feeling of confidence and ease in executing "One," "Two," and "Three" above.

Only at the end of the swing forward, on a line with the skip's broom, at the count of "Three," and just before the release of the stone, the handle is turned. If the 'in turn' (clockwise) has been called for, the point of the stone's handle is turned inward, toward the body, resulting in the palm being turned upward. In the case of the 'out-turn' (counter-clockwise), the point of the handle is turned away from the body, which brings about the release of the stone with the palm down.

NOTE: The length of the slide is not important. This will adjust itself to conform to the build and the ability of the player. The important thing is the "follow-through" (as in golf, tennis and many other sports). Some curlers, especially those of advanced age, prefer to deliver their stones without moving out of the "hack," and many are able to get as good results as the sliders.

**SWEEPING**—Effective broom handling for sweeping purposes is an art in itself. Limited space does not permit an adequate explanation of this important part of the game. Then too, like dancing or skating, the footwork necessary to keep ahead of a fast moving stone, as well as the rhythm and cadence required while swinging the broom, can only be learned on the ice and under the tutelage of an expert. The technique in use also varies according to the stature and build of the player.

19

# CURLING  COURTESY

Courtesy and respect for fellow curlers, opponents and members of your own rink alike, are among the most significant of all curling customs. Important as the game itself is, an understanding of the unwritten Rules Of Good Behavior are essential to the enjoyment of Curling. Following are some of the important things to remember.

1. Never distract a player about to deliver his stone, by talking or moving about. Show him the same courtesy that you will expect when your turn comes to play.

2. It is very disconcerting to the player, for those on the ice ready to sweep to cross over to the other side while the skip is giving instructions to the man in the hack. Decide in advance which side you want to sweep on and remain still until after the stone is on its way.

3. Never fail to compliment even an opponent for making a good shot and, on the other hand, do not embarrass a player by making remarks about an unsuccessful shot.

4. Leads and seconds are not allowed in the goal area until after the completion of an end and score has been determined. It is even customary for the Skip to leave the house while the vice-skips agree upon the score.

5. As their turn comes to play, curlers should be in the hack with stone cleaned and ready to take Skip's instructions as promptly as possible. This speeds up the game materially. Skips, themselves, should keep the game moving by minimizing delay in making their decisions.

6. Confine your attention to your own game rather than watching the play on another sheet. Your enthusiasm and interest in your team's progress has a definite bearing on the outcome of your match.

7. Curling is a gentleman's game — and one where the Golden Rule prevails before, during and after the game. Above all, this tradition should be observed. (See "Spirit of Curling" on back cover.)

# SKIP'S STRATEGY

It is said that skips are born, not made. In any case, "building the house" properly, is a difficult job. So many varied problems are continually occurring. Every end is different. The requisites of a successful skip are a good disposition, alertness, diplomacy and courage, plus a knowledge of the game through experience. Limited space can only allow for a few hints on typical situations which may be helpful.

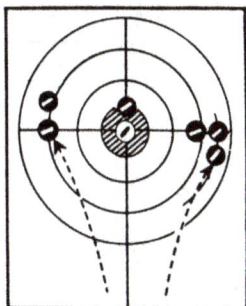

**Best guard is a 2nd shot. Canny to spread shots.**

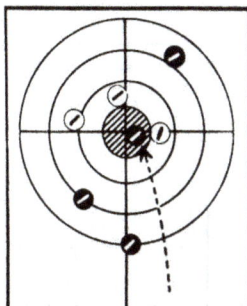

**When in doubt — draw!**

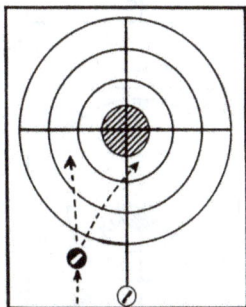

**Play more short raises! (The two-for-one shot.)**

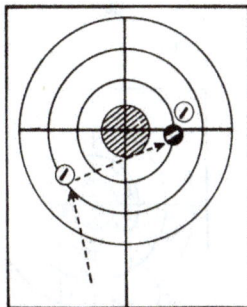

**When hitting . . . Play to remove the front stone first.**

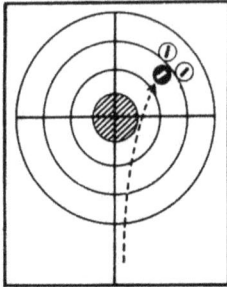

Draw to opposing stones behind the tee . . . Use them
for backing.

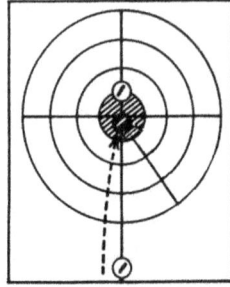

Draw around long guards.

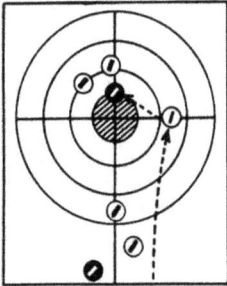

When in trouble . . . play
for a roll!

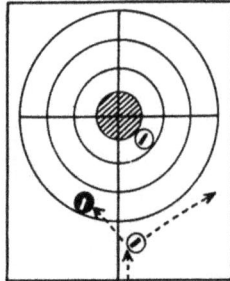

Chip the guard and — roll in
for second.

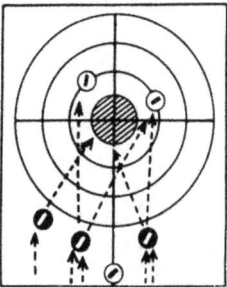

Two-for-one shots are possible
with quiet weight.

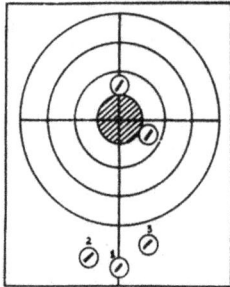

Open up the front and let the
sunshine in. Play to hit No. 1.

22

# COUNTRY CLUBS AND
# OTHER SIMILAR ORGANIZATIONS

Properly organized and promoted, curling can be a cure for "winter-time suffering" from want of revenue, a real "cure" for assessments. It takes a little "doing," however, to work up sufficient enthusiasm as there are few who know anything about the sport, and it calls for some wholesale "selling" before the Board of Governors will give it consideration.

Clubs always have an imposing list of improvements awaiting available funds. Consequently, unless the membership at large can be convinced, a presently little known sport such as curling would never have a chance. The varying temperatures in all parts of the country make artificial ice an essential, and because of snow, rain and bad weather, which upset curling schedules, a suitable building is also necessary. Therefore a proper set-up means a major expenditure—let us say somewhere between $50,000 and $100,000 depending upon the number of "sheets" and the type of building.

Two sheets are sufficient for a total membership of 300 curlers. With five, eight or ten "end" games per day, during the five month's season 1500 games could be played, in which 12,000 players would participate. This would allow each player 40 games per season, or three or more games per week.

Additional revenue to the club during the five winter months (November through March), is sure to absorb such an expenditure (or retire the bond issue) in a very short time, due to the popularity of the sport once it gets going. This has been proven many times in recent years in clubs that have adopted curling. Because of it's unequaled social side, the restaurant and bar can be made to thrive throughout the winter. Then too, it is a small price to pay for the good health and companionship to be enjoyed by all members young and old. Why sit down· by the fire and catch cold, after putting the golf clubs and tennis racquets away?

Experience has proven that the proper procedure to build up interest, is to set up an evening program of curling entertainment following one of the clubs regular buffet dinners. Advance notices to all members can be mailed out announcing the event, which includes a short explanation of the game, followed by some extraordinary professional sound movies of curling played at it's best in the Canadian Championships. (See pages 28 and 29 for further information on how to arrange for such a program and write for complete and convincing Country Club survey.)

If the Board is still not "sold" on the merits of curling as an added income for the club, there is a next move that seldom fails, provided there is a nucleus of at least 20 members who would like to try it out "on a shoestring" at very little expense. Used stones which have been laid aside by going clubs that have purchased new sets, are always obtainable. A small area can be flooded, or a "water hazard" on the golf course utilized for a season's curling experience. True, they will only be able to curl when the weather is favorable, but at least, it would be a start.

## ICE ARENAS & MUNICIPAL ICE RINKS

Many such places, having artificial ice are utilized for skating, hockey and occasional ice shows only. Added revenue may be secured by the use of the ice for curling purposes during certain hours of the day or week—women and children during the daytime, men in the evening and for mixed games during the week-end. Curlers welcome the opportunity of utilizing such ice, as it is far less expensive than paying their share of an artificial ice set-up belonging to their own private club. This can come later.

The ice area of these arenas is usually of standard size, approximately 85x185 feet. This affords space enough for five or six "sheets" when it is used for curling purposes. In other words, six games, for example, can be played simultaneously (accommodating forty-eight players) with a surplus of ice left over measuring 35x85 feet. This may be used at the same time for figure skating, etc.

Practically all of the curling in it's native country, Scotland, is played on indoor ice of this description. Instantly removable "surface hacks" are used in place of embedded ones. This allows skating to take place immediately after the curling games are over, without any interruption or further servicing of the ice.

Often curling clubs, having no facilities of their own, lease the entire area for two and one-half hour intervals (enough time for ten "ends" or innings to be played). At a fee of $3.50 per player (about the same charge as for the use of an indoor bowling alley for the same period), the revenue for the six games would be **$168.00**, not including the income from the left-over area above mentioned. (5 draws per day would gross $840.00.)

In most cases, such arena ice is not completely utilized at all times, so except during hockey games, one or two curling games may be provided for along the sides for use simultaneously with the skating. Then too, all skaters are potential prospects for curling, as they are entrigued by the games which are in progress during the skating period.

## CURLING IN INDUSTRY

Recreation Associations serving industry have been searching for a competitive team sport which can be enjoyed by the entire families of all plant personnel. At present the indoor bowling leagues in the winter and soft ball teams in summer, fall short of fully accomplishing this.

A game which would create companionship and goodwill is sought, where all players have the feeling of equality with one another. Curling could be the answer and certainly should be thoroughly investigated by industrial recreation departments with the thought of launching at least a trial program.

## CURLING IN THE SCHOOLS

Unlike Canada, very little has been done with the sport in U. S. schools. This is purely through lack of knowledge of it's benefits. If ever there was a game qualified to mold a nation's manhood and teach that most difficult of all lessons "How to lose graciously," curling is it! Canadian schools have accepted it's merits as a game which brings unity of purpose through greater understanding of each other—emphasizes the value of teamwork and the importance of sportsmanship.

In the fraternity of curling, no one has done more to bring about its acceptance by the schools, than **Ken** Watson of Winnipeg. Without remuneration, and solely on the strength of his convictions, he has made curling the major pastime in many of the educational institutions throughout the Dominion. There are now close to 75,000 youngsters in Canada who curl—more than participate in any other winter game. It is the only school sport there in which a Canadian Champion is declared.

# INTERIOR FINISH AND PROPER
# LIGHTING OF THE MODERN
# CURLING RINK

If you are going to build a curling rink remember that good visability through the use of a proper color scheme for ceiling, walls and the ice itself, plus an adequate lighting system, is essential to good curling.

Too often these finishing touches to the interior, which generally have no windows or skylights, are neglected. As a rule, by the time consideration is being given to these essentials, all of the money has been used up for the building, the artificial ice equipment, curling stones and other necessary accessories. The tendency then is to "shop around" to find the cheapest way to finish things up. (Write for article, "Where there's light . . . there's hope for better curling.")

In the first place, the interior paint job should be done in one of the attractive lighter colors for the walls such as light green, beige or yellow, with a good, flat white for the ceiling. The ice itself should be made as white as possible. This is done by painting one of the under ice coats with a good white water paint. The lighter colors throughout will give the whole interior a "lift," regardless of the type of artificial lighting equipment used.

Whether the source of light is from incadescent light bulbs or the more modern fluorescent tubes, they should be concealed from the eyes of the players and also the spectators. Good visibility is essential in making accurate shots.

Do not try "trick" color schemes for the ice, even in the goal areas. Remember the greater the contrast between the grey or brown of the curling stone and it's background, the ice, the greater the visability for the player and skip alike.

An even distribution of light over the entire ice area will make it possible for the skips to judge the speed and direction of the stones, nature of the ice etc. The goal areas should be "highlighted" by means of spot or flood lamps concealed above, to an intensity of at least 40 "foot candles"; about three or four times that of the rest of the ice surface.

Don't ruin your curling club by trying to save a few dollars on these finishing touches.

The above illustrates an adequate lighting system. Note
the visibility — the smooth, shadowless illumination — a day-
light effect! For complete details on the lighting equipment
used in this modern curling rink of the Glen View Club, at
Golf, Illinois write to Dar Curtis. (address—last page)

Helpful information can also be supplied on artificial
ice installations and maintenance. Curling ice is always
suitable for skating but requires a little more attention.
The necessary accessories needed for curling such as
"hacks", brooms, measuring devices, score boards, etc.,
are important. Data on these will be furnished on
request.

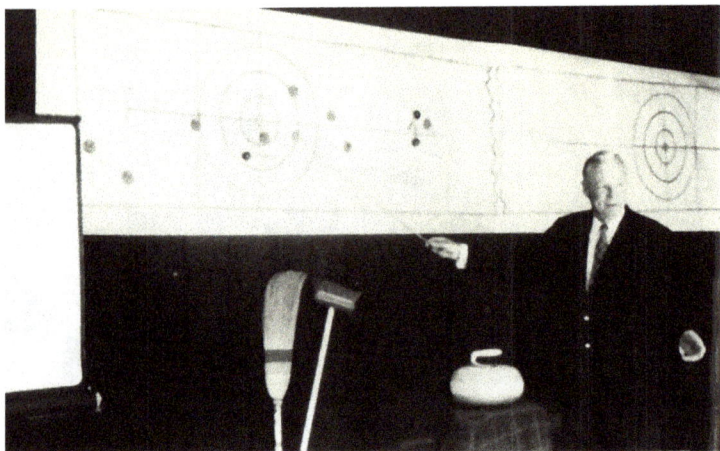

Movable discs representing stones, used on a large "wall chart" help the audience to visualize a game in action.

## ENTERTAINING & PROMOTIONAL SHOW FOR YOUR CLUB OR GROUP

It may be said that those who have read this far have indicated their interest. Space does not permit full coverage of all phases of this fascinating game, so, in the interest of bringing more fun to more people during the long winter months, the services of the **Curtis Curling Clearing House** are available to those who want to know more. All these helps are without charge.

A comprehensive program of from one to two hours duration is offered free to prospective clubs, schools, and other groups, known as the "CHART SHOW". It is not a "lecture", but is entertaining, as well as instructive, and has been given over a hundred times by the author—see photo above.*

A complete library as well as files, photographs, sound movie films, samples of accessories, badges, trophies, songs, poems, speeches etc. have been collected over the past 27 years—all are available without charge.

*The only cost for such a curling program would be my nominal traveling expenses.*

# FILMS YOU CAN BORROW
## FOR YOUR MEETING

1. "PADDY'S MILESTONE"—1200 ft. Made in Scotland. Quarrying granite—mfgr. of curling stones in Kay Co. plant. Outdoor and indoor curling. Followed by: "INDIAN HILL SQUAWS"—400 ft. (silent with captions explaining game). U. S. women curlers in action made by Fox-Movietone.

2. "THE ROARING GAME"—400 ft. with Ken Watson. Instructional film showing—the turns, slide delivery, sweeping, men, women, children curling etc. Followed by: "MACDONALD BRIER"—800 ft. Canadian Championship at Winnipeg.

3. "INDIAN HILL SQUAWS"—400 ft. (Silent film) See above. Followed by: "MACDONALD BRIER"—800 ft. Canadian Championship at Winnipeg.

4. "THERE'S MAGIC IN CURLING"—600 ft. Instructional film with Ken Watson.

5. "SKIP'S DILEMMA"—600 ft. Problems of first year skip with Ken Watson.

6. "THE DRAMA OF CURLING"—1400 ft. Canadian Championship at Moncton.

7. "CANADIAN CURLING CHAMPIONSHIP"—1957 at Kingston, Ontario.

8. "THE VICTORIA BRIER"—1958 Canadian Championship.

9. "LAKEHEAD BRIER"—1960 Canadian Championship (color).

Note: All listed above are 16 mm sound films except parts of Nos. 1 & 3 which are silent.

# THE SPIRIT OF CURLING

The heart of curling is its incomparable spirit. Without that spirit, curling is just another pasttime. Played in that spirit, it is the king of all games. The spirit of curling is reflected in its most cherished traditions.

Curlers play the game to win; but not to humble their opponents. Every curling game ends with a hearty handclasp of friendship and goodwill to both teammates and opponents.

Every true curler would rather lose than win unfairly. He never attempts to distract any opponent or otherwise prevent him from playing his best. No curler ever deliberately breaks a rule of the game; and should he do so inadverently and be aware of it, he is the first to divulge the breach.

From time immemorial curling has been a truly amateur sport. No curler plays the game for pecuniary profit either to himself or any one else.

Uniformity of curling costumes to indicate teams or curling clubs is universally approved; but the advertising of any business or product by such means militates against the amateur spirit of the game.

Prizes of more or less value — and the less the intrinsic value, the better — are awarded for success in the game and are cherished chiefly as mementos. Curling is the kind of game that neither needs nor permits a wager upon its outcome to enhance its enjoyment. Only by a strict observance of these time-honored traditions can curling be kept as a game that is played for love of it alone.

The respect and honor accorded to any curler is derived neither from his wealth not his social positions, but rather from his worth as a man, his skill, gentlemanly conduct as a curler, and his devotion to the game and its spirit.

(Above contributed by "Fergie" Ferguson of Milwaukee, Wis.)

# COACHWHIP PUBLICATIONS

## COACHWHIPBOOKS.COM

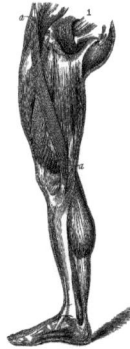

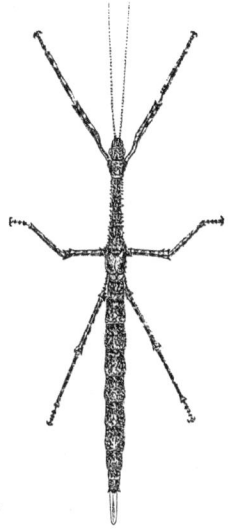

www.ingramcontent.com/pod-product-compliance
Lightning Source LLC
Chambersburg PA
CBHW071941020426
42331CB00010B/2964